THE MUSCULAR SYSTEM

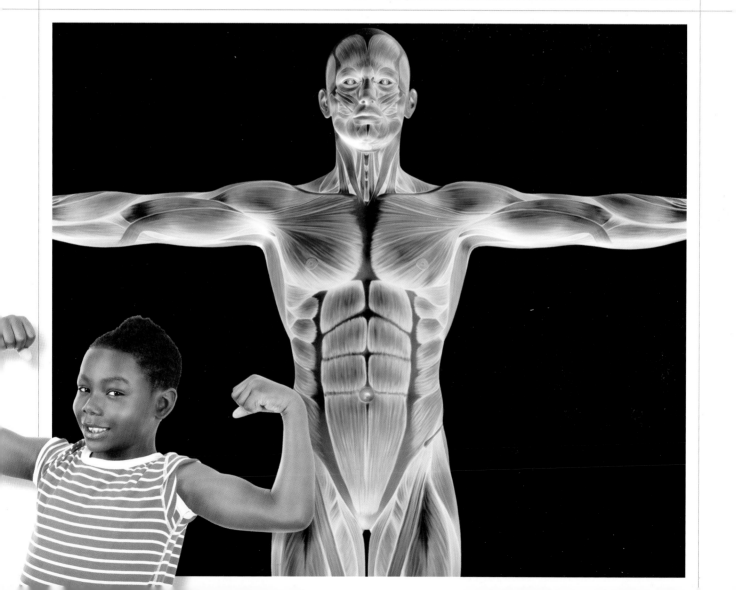

Published by The Child's World®
1980 Lookout Drive • Mankato, MN 56003-1705
800-599-READ • www.childsworld.com

Acknowledgments
The Child's World®: Mary Berendes, Publishing Director
Red Line Editorial: Editorial direction
The Design Lab: Design
Amnet: Production

Content Consultant: R. John Solaro, Ph.D., Distinguished
University Professor and Head, Department of Physiology and
Biophysics, University of Illinois Chicago

Photographs ©: Shutterstock Images, cover (background),
1 (background), 14; Sanjay Deva/Shutterstock Images, cover
(foreground), 1 (foreground); Nate Allred/Shutterstock Images,
4; BlueRingMedia/Shutterstock Images, 7; Jupiterimages/
Thinkstock, 8; iStockphoto/Thinkstock, 11, 12; Monkey Business
Images/Thinkstock, 17; Wong Sze Yuen/Shutterstock Images,
19; Wavebreak Media/Shutterstock Images, 20

ISBN 9781626873360
LCCN 2014930673

Printed in the United States of America
Mankato, MN
July, 2014
PA02221

ABOUT THE AUTHOR

Susan H. Gray has a bachelor's and a master's degree in zoology. In her 25 years as an author, she has written many medical articles, grant proposals, and children's books. Ms. Gray and her husband, Michael, live in Cabot, Arkansas.

TABLE OF CONTENTS

CHAPTER 1

Jeremy Proves Himself

"Hey, Jeremy! Show us your muscles!" Jeremy's big brothers were trying to prove how strong they were. One brother did six push-ups. The other brother grabbed a tree limb and did a pull-up.

Your muscles help you move and play. They even help you pull yourself up to hang from a tree branch!

Jeremy shouted back, "Watch this!" He ran over to a concrete block and dug his fingertips under it. Jeremy tried to stand up. His body grew tense. Electrical signals shot through his nerves. A special chemical flowed out of the nerves going to his muscle cells. The chemical made thousands of Jeremy's muscle cells try to shorten.

Jeremy slowly rose with the block in his hands. More muscle cells shortened. Jeremy stood up straight and lifted the block to his chest. His arm muscles were bulging. And his legs were trembling. Jeremy dropped the block on the ground.

Jeremy's brothers were impressed. Jeremy's legs and arms were hurting. He had no energy left. Jeremy had certainly shown his muscles.

DID YOU KNOW?

Some people believe exercise turns fat cells into muscle cells. This is not true. With exercise, you can build up your muscle cells while fat cells shrink in size.

CHAPTER 2

What Is the Muscular System?

There are three kinds of muscle tissue in the body. Smooth muscle lies inside the walls of blood vessels and some of the organs. The heart is made of **cardiac muscle**. **Skeletal muscles** are the ones we usually think of as muscles. They are in the arms, legs, back, neck, face, chest, and abdomen. These muscles help us move. They also help us sit and stand without falling over.

Sometimes skeletal muscles go by other names. They are often called striated muscles. Striations are little stripes. Under a microscope, skeletal muscles appear to have many striations. Skeletal muscles are also called voluntary muscles. If something is voluntary, that means we have control. We can control the movements of voluntary muscles. Involuntary muscles work without us telling them to.

The heart is a special kind of involuntary muscle. Other involuntary muscles are found in the lungs and blood vessels.

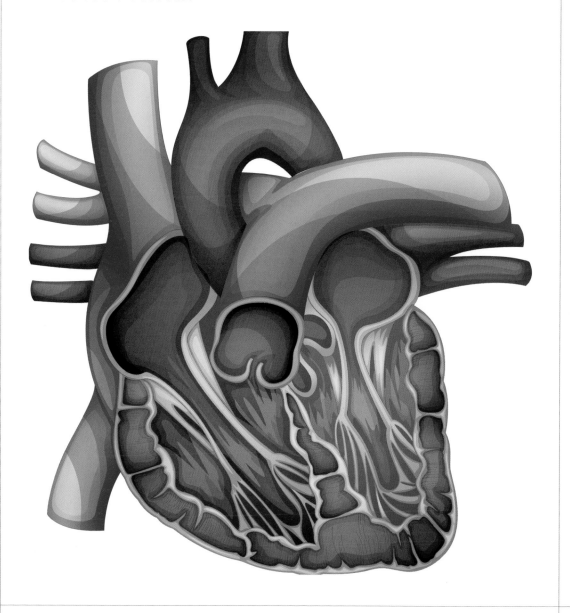

The cardiac muscle is only found in the heart.

All muscle tissue can do four things. It can extend, or stretch. It also contracts, or shortens. Muscle tissue always returns to its normal size. Muscles react to chemicals in their environment. The chemicals come from nerve tips and cause muscles to contract.

Muscles also react to electricity. Sometimes a person whose heart is not beating normally goes to the hospital. The doctor can give the heart muscle an electrical shock. If things work right, the heart reacts to the shock. It stops beating for just a moment. Then it starts beating normally.

Even after stretching, your muscles will always return to their normal length.

CHAPTER 3

What Are the Parts of a Muscle?

Muscle is really the "meat" of the body. When you eat chicken, you are eating bird muscles. When you eat tuna, you are eating muscle tissue from the fish. In many animals, muscles form a large part of the body. Muscles make up approximately 30 to 50 percent of a human's weight.

Voluntary muscles are loaded with blood vessels and nerves. Blood brings food and oxygen to muscles so they can work. Blood also takes away waste materials.

Muscles are made up of many tiny cells. Each cell is equal to or smaller in diameter than a human hair. However, cells can be several feet long. Muscle cells are also called muscle fibers. Nerves run from the spinal cord out to the muscles. The spinal cord is a thick bundle of nerves running down the back.

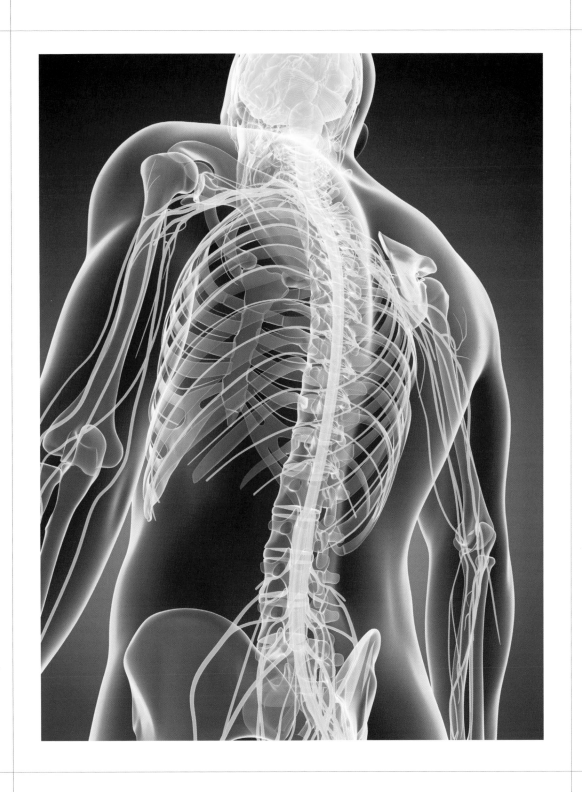

*Your muscles are connected to your brain
through the spinal cord.*

It connects the brain to the muscles. When the nerves reach the muscles, they split into many branches. Each branch comes to an end right on a muscle fiber.

Skeletal muscles have at least two ends. One end is anchored to a bone. The other end is attached to another bone or a tissue. The tough cord that attaches a muscle to a bone is called a **tendon**.

Muscles have all kinds of shapes. Some of the muscles in the back are wide sheets of tissue.

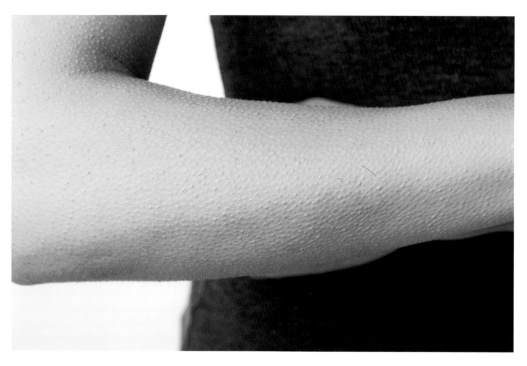

Your muscles are even working when you have goose bumps!

Circular muscles surround the eyes and mouth. When you pucker your lips, the circular muscle around your mouth contracts. When you close your eyes tightly, the circular muscles around your eyes go to work. Most muscles are in the shape of straps or bands. The muscles that make your eyes roll are such muscles.

CHAPTER 4

How Can Muscles Make You Move?

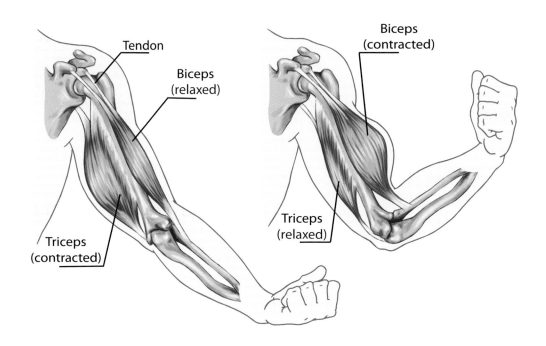

Tendon

Biceps
(relaxed)

Biceps
(contracted)

Triceps
(contracted)

Triceps
(relaxed)

There are about 650 voluntary muscles in the body. They give the body its shape. They also help you move in every way you can imagine. Muscles in the hips, legs, feet, and toes help you run. Muscles

*When you flex your arm, your
bicep muscle contracts.*

around the eyes make you squint. Muscles in the arm move your fingers.

You move because your muscles contract. They develop a force or tension. A muscle pulls on a body part when it contracts. When it pulls, that body part moves.

Try this yourself. Point your foot down. Notice how your **calf muscle** contracts and hardens. When the muscle contracted, it pulled your heel bone up. Now point your foot up. To do this, the muscles on the front of your leg contracted. They pulled your foot up. You can even feel the muscles harden as they do so.

You have just seen how muscles work in pairs. One muscle pulls a body part one way. Another muscle pulls it the opposite way. Muscles never push body parts—they always pull.

CHAPTER 5

What Makes a Muscle Contract?

For a whole muscle to contract, many tiny muscle cells must contract at once. When it is time for a muscle to move, the nerve endings go into action. They release a special chemical. The chemical causes the fibers to contract. When many fibers contract at once, the whole muscle contracts. Lifting a feather only activates a few muscle cells. Lifting a heavy backpack activates many cells.

When it is time for a muscle to relax, another chemical comes along. It stops the action of the first chemical. This allows the fibers to relax and return to their normal size.

DID YOU KNOW?
When people feel cold, they shiver. This is a muscle activity that produces heat. It is a way that muscles work to keep the body warm.

Just imagine what happens every time you move. Millions of nerve endings put out chemicals. The chemicals make millions of tiny fibers contract. All of those little contractions make whole muscles contract. The muscles pull on body parts to make them move.

CHAPTER 6

Healthy and Unhealthy Muscles

The muscular system keeps you moving. It is important to keep the system healthy. A healthy muscular system needs plenty of water and the right foods. High-protein foods help build and repair muscle tissue. Such foods include eggs, milk, meat, fish, and nuts.

Muscles need **carbohydrates** for energy. Bread, cereal, crackers, and potatoes contain these. Calcium and potassium are important for nerves to work properly. They also keep muscles from cramping. Calcium is in milk, cheese, and yogurt. Potassium is in bananas.

Sometimes, the muscular system becomes diseased. Even with proper nutrition, the muscles might not get better. Muscular dystrophy is one

Drinking milk helps keep your body healthy.

such disease. Over time, the muscles become weaker and less able to function.

Myasthenia gravis is another muscular disease. The body will not let the nerve chemicals do their job. Muscles cannot contract properly. A person with this disease might have trouble talking, swallowing, or moving.

Scientists are looking at how healthy and diseased muscles work. They are studying nerve chemicals. They are looking at the molecules deep

Scientists are learning more everyday about how our muscles work.

inside muscle fibers.
Scientists are looking at
how damaged muscle
repairs itself. They are
learning more about how
exercise and diet affect
muscles. Scientists have
come a long way since
they first began studying
muscles. However, there is still plenty to learn.

GLOSSARY

calf muscle (KAF MUHSS-uhl) The calf muscle is in the back part of the lower leg. The calf muscle contracts when you point your foot down.

carbohydrates (KAR-bo-HY-drates) Carbohydrates are types of food that are built out of sugars. Muscles need carbohydrates for energy.

cardiac muscle (KAR-dee-ak MUHSS-uhl) The cardiac muscle is an involuntary muscle that makes up the heart. Your body only has one cardiac muscle.

skeletal muscles (SKELL-uh-tul MUHSS-uhls) Skeletal muscles are muscles usually attached to the skeleton. Skeletal muscles are found almost everywhere in the body, including the back, the neck, and the face.

tendon (TEN-duhn) A tendon is a tough piece of tissue that connects muscle to the bone. Lower arm muscles have a long tendon connecting them to the fingers.

LEARN MORE

BOOKS

Gardner, Jane P. *Take a Closer Look at Your Muscles*.
Mankato, MN: The Child's World, 2014.

Manolis, Kay. *The Muscular System*.
Minneapolis: Bellwether Media, 2009.

Slike, Janet. *Take a Closer Look at Your Heart*.
Mankato, MN: The Child's World, 2014.

WEB SITES

Visit our Web site for links about the muscular system:
childsworld.com/links

Note to Parents, Teachers, and Librarians: We routinely verify our
Web links to make sure they are safe and active sites.
So encourage your readers to check them out!

INDEX